MW01206153

100

Positive Quotes About Doing Your Best

Jesse Worth

Copyright © 2023 Jesse Worth

All rights reserved.

ISBN: 9798398192933
Imprint: Independently published

<u>DEDICATION</u>

This book is dedicated to all those who strive to make a positive difference in their own lives and in the lives of others. May these quotes be a guiding light, a source of comfort, and a reminder that even in the midst of challenges, there is always something to be grateful for.

With boundless appreciation and admiration,

Jesse Worth

Your Review Matters

Your review could really help us get the word out about this book. Please take the time to leave a review. Use the QR Code below to access the Amazon review form.

Thank you for your support!

CONTENTS

100 Positive Quotes About Doing Your Best

QUOTE #1

"Do the best you can until you know better. Then when you know better, do better."

-Maya Angelou

QUOTE #2

"Success is not final, failure is not fatal. It is the courage to continue that counts."

-Winston Churchill

QUOTE #3

"It is easier to build strong children than to repair broken men."

-Frederick Douglass

QUOTE #4

"The secret of getting ahead is getting started. The secret of getting started is breaking your complex, overwhelming tasks into small, manageable tasks, and then starting on the first one."

-Mark Twain

QUOTE #5

"Don't watch the clock; do what it does.
Keep going."

-Sam Levenson

QUOTE #6

"Believe you can and you're halfway there."

-Theodore Roosevelt

QUOTE #7

"The most effective way to do it is to do it."

-Amelia Earhart

QUOTE #8

"You are never too old to set another goal or to dream a new dream."

-C.S. Lewis

QUOTE #9

"The harder the conflict, the greater the triumph."

-George Washington

QUOTE #10

"The harder you work, the harder it is to surrender."

-Vince Lombardi

QUOTE #11

"The greatest glory in living lies not in never falling, but in rising every time we fall."

-Nelson Mandela

QUOTE #12

"We can complain because rose bushes have thorns, or rejoice because thorns have roses."

-Abraham Lincoln

QUOTE #13

"No matter what people tell you, words and ideas can change the world."

-Robin Williams

QUOTE #14

"Let no one ever come to you without leaving better and happier."

-Mother Teresa

QUOTE #15

"Do not put off until tomorrow what can be done today."

-Thomas Jefferson

QUOTE #16

"If you want something you've never had, you must be willing to do something you've never done."

-Thomas Jefferson

QUOTE #17

"Success is no accident. It is hard work, perseverance, learning, studying, sacrifice, and most of all, love of what you are doing or learning to do."

-Pele

QUOTE #18

"The time is always right to do what is right."

-Martin Luther King, Jr.

QUOTE #19

"The longer I live, the more beautiful life
becomes."

-Frank Lloyd Wright

QUOTE #20

"When everything seems to be going against
you, remember that the airplane takes off
against the wind, not with it."

-Henry Ford

QUOTE #21

"A problem is a chance for you to do your best."

-Duke Ellington

QUOTE #22

"Work is love made visible."

-Khalil Bibran

QUOTE #23

"Success is not the absence of problems; it's the ability to deal with them."

-Steve Maraboli

QUOTE #24

"Luck is what happens when preparation meets opportunity."

-Seneca

QUOTE #25

"The positive thinker sees opportunity in every difficulty."

-Winston Churchill

QUOTE #26

"Be the best version of yourself in anything you do. You don't have to live anybody else's story."

-Dawn Staley

QUOTE #27

"Even in the darkest places, the human spirit
can rise above any circumstance."

-Nelson Mandela

QUOTE #28

"The best revenge is massive success."

-Frank Abagnale

QUOTE #29

"Don't be discouraged by a failure. It can be a positive experience. Failure is, in a sense, the highway to success, inasmuch as every discovery of what is false leads us to seek earnestly after what is true, and every fresh experience points out some form of error which we shall afterward carefully avoid."

-John Keats

QUOTE #30

"No person was ever wise by chance."

-Seneca

QUOTE #31

"Always be yourself, express yourself, have faith in yourself, do not go out and look for a successful personality and duplicate it."

-Bruce Lee

QUOTE #32

"Remember that failure is an event, not a person."

-Zig Ziglar

QUOTE #33

"The best way to predict your future is to create it."

-Peter Drucker

QUOTE #34

"You can't get much done in life if you only work on the days when you feel good."

-Pat Summitt

QUOTE #35

"Choose to be optimistic. It feels better."

-Dalai Lama

QUOTE #36

"Losing is a learning experience. It teaches you humility. It teaches you to work harder. It's also a powerful motivator."

-Yogi Berra

QUOTE #37

"The greatest test of courage is to bear defeat without losing heart."

-Robert Green Ingersoll

QUOTE #38

"Success is a project that's always under construction."

-Pat Summitt

QUOTE #39

"Do not look for approval except for the consciousness of doing your best."

-Andrew Carnegie

QUOTE #40

"It's not the will to win that matters – everyone has that. It's the will to prepare to win that matters."

-Paul "Bear" Bryant

QUOTE #41

"You never know how strong you are until being strong is your only choice."

-Bob Marley

QUOTE #42

"The difference between successful people and others is how long they spend time feeling sorry for themselves."

-Meg Whitman

QUOTE #43

"The more positive thoughts you entertain,
the happier you will become."

-Rhonda Byrne

QUOTE #44

"You miss 100% of the shots you don't take."

-Wayne Gretzky

QUOTE #45

"Don't limit yourself. Many people limit themselves to what they think they can do. You can go as far as your mind lets you. What you believe, remember, you can achieve."

-Mary Kay Ash

QUOTE #46

"Do your best, and then let life do the rest."

-Conan O'Brien

QUOTE #47

"Keep your face always toward the sunshine –
and shadows will fall behind you."

-Walt Whitman

QUOTE #48

"Do not mistake activity for achievement."

-John Wooden

QUOTE #49

"Failure is the condiment that gives success its flavor."

-Truman Capote

QUOTE #50

"Don't be afraid to give up the good to go for the great."

-John D. Rockefeller

QUOTE #51

"The greatest waste in the world is the difference between what we are and what we could become."

-Andrew Mellon

QUOTE #52

"Look at a day when you are supremely satisfied at the end. It's not a day when you lounge around doing nothing; it's when you've had everything to do, and you've done it."

-Margaret Thatcher

QUOTE #53

"I got my start by giving myself a start."

-C.J. Walker

QUOTE #54

"The difference between the impossible and the possible lies in a person's determination."

-Tommy Lasorda

QUOTE #55

"Here's how I'm going to beat you. I'm going to outwork you. That's it. That's all there is to it."

-Pat Summitt

QUOTE #56

"Pessimism never won any battle."

-Dwight Eisenhower

QUOTE #57

"Go as far as you can see; when you get there, you'll be able to see further."

-J.P. Morgan

QUOTE #58

"To be successful, you must decide exactly what you want to accomplish, then resolve to pay the price to get it."

-Kim Mulkey

QUOTE #59

"Don't be pushed around by the fears in your mind. Be led by the dreams in your heart."

-Roy T. Bennett

QUOTE #60

"It's hard to beat a person who never gives up."

-Babe Ruth

QUOTE #61

"Positive thinking will let you do everything
better than negative thinking will."

-Zig Ziglar

QUOTE #62

"Experience is the teacher of all things."

-Julius Caesar

QUOTE #63

"Many of life's failures are people who did not realize how close they were to success when they gave up."

-Thomas Edison

QUOTE #64

"The best way to find yourself is to lose yourself in the service of others."

-Mahatma Gandhi

QUOTE #65

"We can't help everyone, but everyone can help someone."

-Ronald Reagan

QUOTE #66

"Losing feels worse than winning feels good."

-Vin Scully

QUOTE #67

"The happiness of your life depends upon the quality of your thoughts."

-Marcus Aurelius

QUOTE #68

"When the going gets tough, the tough get going."

-Joseph P. Kennedy

QUOTE #69

"Failure is the only opportunity to begin again, only this time more wisely."

-Henry Ford

QUOTE #70

"The sky is not the limit, your mind is."

-Nicole Stott

QUOTE #71

"It's not what happens to you, but how you react to it that matters."

-Epictetus

QUOTE #72

"The first step towards getting somewhere is to decide that you are not going to stay where you are."

-J.P. Morgan

QUOTE #73

"He who fears death will never do anything
worthy of a living man."

-Seneca

QUOTE #74

"If there is no struggle, there is no progress."

-Frederick Douglass

QUOTE #75

"The future depends on what you do today."

-Mahatma Gandhi

QUOTE #76

"I have not failed. I've just found 10,000 ways that won't work."

-Thomas Edison

QUOTE #77

"The only limit to our realization of tomorrow will be our doubts of today."

-Franklin D. Roosevelt

QUOTE #78

"The harder you work, the harder it is to surrender."

-Marv Levy

QUOTE #79

"Don't seek for everything to happen as you wish it would, but rather wish that everything happens as it actually will – then your life will flow well."

-Epictetus

QUOTE #80

"Do the best you can in every task, no matter how unimportant it may seem at the time. No one learns more about a problem than the person at the bottom."

-Sandra Day O'Connor

QUOTE #81

"Courage is being scared to death and saddling up anyway."

-John Wayne

QUOTE #82

"In the end, it's not about what you say, it's about what you do."

-Eric Olson

QUOTE #83

"It's not enough to do your best, you must know what to do, then do your best."

-W. Edwards Deming

QUOTE #84

"Gratitude can transform common days into thanksgivings, turn routine jobs into joy, and change ordinary opportunities into blessings."

-William Arthur Ward

QUOTE #85

"Do not let your mind become entangled in things you cannot control or change. Focus instead on what you can do, and do it to the best of your abilities."

-Marcus Aurelius

QUOTE #86

"Never give up, because you never know if the next try is going to be the one that works."

-Sally Ride

QUOTE #87

"Efforts and courage are not enough without purpose and direction."

-John F. Kennedy

QUOTE #88

"Do what you feel in your heart to be right – for you'll be criticized anyway."

-Eleanor Roosevelt

QUOTE #89

"We suffer more often in imagination than in reality."

-Seneca

QUOTE #90

"You have to make it happen."

-Margaret Thatcher

QUOTE #91

"Success is not the key to happiness.
Happiness is the key to success. If you love
what you are doing, you will be successful."

-Ray Kelly

QUOTE #92

"Every accomplishment starts with the
decision to try."

-John F. Kennedy

QUOTE #93

"The ultimate measure of a man is not where he stands in moments of comfort and convenience, but where he stands at times of challenge and controversy."

-Martin Luther King, Jr.

QUOTE #94

"Do your best, and be grateful for the opportunity to do so."

-Joe Vitale

QUOTE #95

"Life is either a daring adventure or nothing at all."

-Helen Keller

QUOTE #96

"The only man who never makes a mistake is the man who never does anything."

-Theodore Roosevelt

QUOTE #97

"Optimism is the faith that leads to achievement."

-Helen Keller

QUOTE #98

"Old age is not a defeat; it is a victory, a triumph of survival."

-Maggie Kuhn

QUOTE #99

"Success comes from knowing that you did your best to become the best that you are capable of becoming."

-John Wooden

QUOTE #100

"It is not that we have a short time to live, but that we waste a lot of it."

-Seneca

CLOSING THOUGHTS

There are several common themes in the quotes selected. Setbacks and failures are part of life's journey and can be catalysts for personal growth and future success.

It is important to do our best in every situation, regardless of external circumstances.

By doing your best, you inspire others.

LOOKING FOR MORE?

AVAILABLE NOW AT

AMAZON.COM

Made in United States
North Haven, CT
08 July 2025

70461657R10036